Copyright © 2015
All rights reserved. This book or any por
may not be reproduced or used in any manner whatsoever
without the express written permission of the publisher
except for the use of brief quotations in a book review.
All pictures are under creative common license by db.everkinetic.com

Other Books By Felix Harder

Click On The Cover To Go To The Book

"The fitness and nutrition world is a breeding ground for obsessive-compulsive behavior. The irony is that many of the things people worry about have no impact on results either way, and therefore aren't worth an ounce of concern."

- Alan Aragon

TABLE OF CONTENTS

INTRODUCTION – WHO THIS BOOK IS FOR	6
THE 80/20 RULE EXPLAINED	8
THE 80/20 RULE IN FITNESS AND BODYBUILDING	10
APPLYING THE 80/20 RULE TO EXERCISE – HOW TO BUILD MUSCLE AND LOSE FAT	12
EXERCISE SELECTION - THE IMPORTANCE OF COMPOUND EXERCISES	14
WARM UP AND THINGS TO KEEP IN MIND BEFORE EVERY WORKOUT	18
SAMPLE WORKOUT	19
APPLYING THE 80/20 RULE TO NUTRITION – WHAT MAKES A GOOD DIET	26
5 MOST IMPORTANT FACTORS FOR A SUCCESSFUL DIET	28
MACRONUTRIENTS EXPLAINED	31
Carbohydrates ("carbs"):	32
Proteins:	34
Fats:	37
APPLYING THE 80/20 RULE TO RECOVERY	42
THE 80/20 RULE IN BODYBUILDING - SUMMARY	44
ALL EXERCISES EXPLAINED:	45
Chest	46
Bench Press	47
Incline Bench Press	50
Decline Bench Press	53

Back	56
Deadlift	57
Lat Pulldown	60
Bent Over Barbell Row	63
Pull-up	66
Legs	69
Barbell Squat	70
Leg Press	73
Dumbbell Lunges	76
Shoulders	79
Seated Barbell Military Press / Shoulder Press	80
Arms	83
Chin Up	84
Triceps Dip	87

Introduction – Who This Book Is For

I wrote this book for people who lead a busy lifestyle but still want to build muscle and get in shape. By giving you the necessary tools to reach your fitness goals, I will have to debunk some training myths that have been around for decades. How many times has someone told me that if I wanted to build muscle I had to...

Hit the gym at least five times per week...

Workout three or even four hours...

Drink two or more protein shakes per day...

And perfectly time my meals no more than three hours apart.

After doing some real research, I quickly learned that most of these "tips" are nonsense and some will even work against you in the long run. I also learned that 80% of muscle building and losing fat could be achieved through only 20% effort. This phenomenon is described as the 80/20 Rule, something that occurs all throughout our lives and not only in bodybuilding. It has completely changed the way I look at my workout. The following chapters will show you how much easier and less time consuming your exercise and dieting routine can be if you focus on a few critical factors and leave the rest to the wannabe experts.

- Felix Harder

The 80/20 Rule Explained

The 80/20 Rule (also known as the Pareto principle) is simple, yet very powerful. It states that, for many events, roughly 80% of the effects come from 20% of the causes. Originally, this rule of thumb referred to the observation that 80% of Italy's wealth belonged to only 20% of the population, made by the Italian Economist Vilfredo Pareto.

Over the years Pareto and other scholars found that this rule seemed to apply to most things in life, for example that:

- 20% of the input creates 80% of the result
- 20% of the customers create 80% of the revenue
- 20% of the workers produce 80% of the result
- 20% of the features cause 80% of the usage

And on and on...

Unfortunately the 80/20 Rule and its applications vanished from popular science during the next centuries and were only "rediscovered" towards the end of the 20th century when top managers found out that the 80/20 rule is dramatically effective when applied to marketing and selling situations. They encouraged their employees to focus their energy towards activity that usually produces very fast and substantial improvements. The later success of these managers and their companies proved the 80/20 Rule to be an extremely useful model with countless applications in various areas of modern life.

The 80/20 Rule In Fitness And Bodybuilding

Pareto's Principle has been successfully used in bodybuilding for more than three decades. Most of the time though, the athletes didn't actually know they were applying a century old "business rule" to their everyday workouts. They simply wanted to <u>get the most out of their training with the least amount of effort.</u> The value of the 80/20 Rule is that it reminds you to focus on the 20% that really matters. Once you have identified these critical factors, you can expect faster than usual muscle growth and/or fat loss with just a few important exercises and a handful of simple diet strategies.

In bodybuilding, what are the 20% that matter?

- Setting up and following a straightforward workout.
- Trainingconsistently and with high intensity
- Following the rule of progressive overload (meaning over time you will lift more weight, more reps or more sets).
- Following a good diet with proper nutrition.
- Getting enough rest for recovery.

In short this means: Train hard, eat well and rest enough. Repeat. If you focus on the basics you will get 80% of the results. Afterwards you only have to adjust your plan every so often, based on your personal experiences and progress.

Applying The 80/20 Rule To Exercise – How To Build Muscle And Lose Fat

If your goal is to build strength and muscle, then it should be rather obvious that most of your time in the gym should be spent lifting weights. Of course, some sort of cardiovascular exercise should always be part of any well-rounded workout, but for the beginner looking to "get big", weight training is essential to increasingstrengthand developing skeletal muscle tissue. Yourfocus should be on lifting progressively heavier weights, with cardio and conditioning as the back-up priorities.

For workouts designed to lose fat, this focus shifts slightly due to the stress that the lower calorie intake puts on your body. Cardio now plays a bigger role in your workout. However, you should still lift heavy when looking to lose fat, otherwise, you risk also losing hard earned muscle mass. The concept of progressive overload, one of the most important pillars of successful bodybuilding states that (only) progressively lifting heavy weights or more reps lead to an increase of muscle strength and size. If you don't provide your body with adequate amounts of stress it will have no incentive to change. Therefore consistent progression is essential to achievingoptimal results. When dieting your progression might be slower, but never lose your effort to progress and increase your weightsover time.

Exercise Selection - The Importance Of Compound Exercises

Oftentimes beginners are confused by the sheer amount of workouts and exercises that it can make it hard for them to see the bigger picture. When looking at the 80/20 principle while trying to combine the most efficient exercises, it becomes obvious that compound exercises are the best way to go. Compound movements utilize multiple joints (usually with free weights instead of machines). They give you the highest yield measured by the time you spend training, which is why your workout should consist mostly of these essential exercises. Always begin your workout with compound exercises that match whatever muscle group you are training that day. This way you achieve maximal muscle recruitment, more nervous system activation, and a bigger stimulus for growth.

Here is a list of the best compound exercises for each muscle group. You can find a detailed description of all exercises at the end of the book under "All Exercises".

<u>Chest:</u>
- Barbell/Dumbbell Bench Press
- Incline Bench Press
- Decline Bench Press

<u>Back:</u>
- Deadlifts
- Pull Ups
- Lat Pulldowns
- Rows (all variations)

<u>Legs:</u>
- Squats
- Leg Press
- (Dumbbell) Lunges

Shoulders:
- Military Press
- Dumbbell Press (all variations)
- Handstand Push Ups

Biceps:
- Chin Ups
- Barbell Biceps Curl

Triceps:
- Dips
- Triceps Bench Press (Narrow Grip)

An example: If you're doing your back and biceps routine today, begin by doing Barbell Rows and Pull Ups for your back muscles and add Chin Ups and Barbell Curls to target your biceps. This way you can create a workout that entirely utilizes compound movements. Such a workout will cause you to suck wind and sweat a lot, because it involves all the muscles in your back and biceps including the many small, stabilizing muscle groups. Therefore, two exercises per targeted muscle group are enough to force your body into muscle growth.

Ultimately, there are countless ways you can structure your workouts but I recommend you spend at least 75% of your time doing compound exercises. Here you can best implement the concept of progressive overload, which we talked about earlier. When doing isolation movements, use them as finishing exercises. They require less total body strength and can help you work an already tired muscle.

Warm Up And Things To Keep In Mind Before Every Workout

Warm Up:
Warm ups are a good way to prevent injuries and help the muscle perform at its maximum. The increased blood flow will also keep your muscles sustained with nutrients. Most trainers recommend getting on the treadmill, cross trainer or exercise bicycle for 5-10 minutes before working out. Before your first exercise you should also do a warm up set (10-15 repetitions) with only the barbell to further warm up the specific muscle group.

Before every workout:
Be sure to eat plenty of carbohydrates so your body can lift at maximum strength. Your last meal should be maximum 1.5 - 2 hours before your training session.

Sample Workout

This is a sample workout, which wasdesigned according to the 80/20 Rule. You will train three times a week and more than 75% of the exercises involve compound movements. Each workout involves only four exercises, all of which will work not only your targeted muscle group but also nearby stabilizing muscles and your core.

<u>Schedule:</u>
Monday - Gym Day 1
Tuesday - Rest
Wednesday - Gym Day 2
Thursday - Rest
Friday - Gym Day 3
Saturday - Rest
Sunday –Rest

Day 1 – Chest/Triceps/Abs

Chest:

Exercise 1: Barbell Bench Press
Sets: 4 (plus 1 Warm Up set)
Reps: 6 – 8 (with heavy weight)

Exercise 2: Incline Dumbbell Bench Press
Sets: 4
Reps: 6 – 8 (with heavy weight)

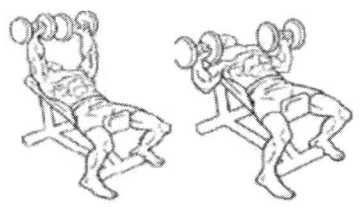

Triceps:

Exercise 3: Triceps Dip
Sets: 5
Reps: 6– 8 (use a weight belt if otherwise too easy)

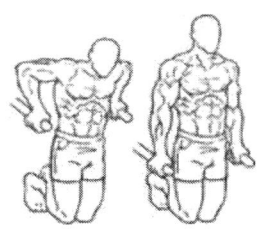

Abs:

Exercise 4: Hanging Leg Raise
Sets: 5
Reps: 8 - 10

Day 2 – Back / Biceps

Back:

Exercise 1: Bent Over Barbell Row
Sets: 4 (plus 1 Warm Up set)
Reps: 6 – 8 (with heavy weight)

Exercise 2: Wide Grip Pull-Ups
Sets: 4
Reps: 6 – 8 (use a weight belt if otherwise too easy)

Biceps:

Exercise 3: Chin-Ups
Sets: 4
Reps: 6 – 8 (use a weight belt if otherwise too easy)

Exercise 4: Hammer Curls
Sets: 4
Reps: 8 – 10

Day 3 – Legs / Shoulders / Abs

Legs:

Exercise 1: Squats
Sets: 4 (Plus 1 Warm Up set)
Reps: 6 – 8 (with heavy weight)

Exercise 2: Dumbbell Lunges
Sets: 4
Reps: 6 – 8

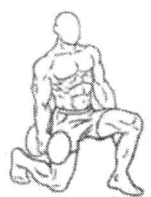

Shoulder:

Exercise 3: Military Press
Sets: 4 (Plus 1 Warm Up set)
Reps: 8 – 10 (with medium weight)

Abs:

Exercise 4: Twisting Crunches
Sets: 5
Reps: 8 – 10

Applying The 80/20 Rule To Nutrition – What Makes A Good Diet

You have probably heard that the right nutrition is more important than the right workout. Well, it's true. If you don't give your muscles the necessary tools for a proper recovery and growth, then they won't get bigger or stronger. As all bodybuilders know, you will never see any significant gains if you aren't eating sufficient amounts of high quality food. Likewise, if you constantly eat at or above your maintenance caloric needs, you can't expect your body to get rid of excess fat. Nutrition is about providing nourishment to your body. The human body needs proper nourishment for the maintenance of our body (muscles, bone, tissues, etc.) and muscle growth. So how do you provide your body with proper nutrition? And how does the 80/20 rule help us decide which diet is the best for our personal fitness goals?

Year of studies done by scientists with the help of athletes and coaches have resulted in a general consensus on what dietary strategies work the best to grow muscle and burn fat. Some of these strategies are fundamental and necessary to see any kind of results, while others will have only minor effects on the successful outcome of your diet. In theory you should follow all of these strategies, but you will see that in practice it can sometimes be almost impossible to stay 100% on point – especially if you lead a busy lifestyle.

5 Most Important Factors for A Successful Diet

In theory there are five simple diet principles that will have a measurable impact on your diet success (see *The Renaissance Diet* by Dr. Mike Israetel). They are:

Caloric Balance (determines around 50% of your diet success):
This principle refers to the number of calories you consume compared to the number of calories your body burns. It determines whether you gain weight, lose weight or maintain weight over time, but does not take into account where the calories come from (carbohydrates, proteins or fats).

Macronutrient Intake (determines around 30% of your diet success):
Macronutrient intake looks at the amount of carbohydrates, protein and fat you take in per day and in what proportion they stand to each other. For anyfixed energy intake, increases in one macronutrient necessarily imply a decrease in the proportion of the other macronutrients. As an example, a high protein diet is usually relatively low in carbohydrates and/or fats.

Nutrient Timing (determines around 10% of your diet success):

Nutrient timing includes the planning of your meals throughout the day, the total amount of meals eaten per day and how you time them in relation to your fitness activity.

Food Composition (determines around 5% of your diet success):
Food composition describes the analysis of the nutrients in a given food such as vitamins and minerals and types of fats. This information can be used to optimize diets and make sure no deficiencies occur.

Dietary Supplements (determine around 5% of your diet success):
Dietary supplements are intended to provide nutrients that you may otherwise not consume in sufficient quantities. Among others, they generally include vitamins pills, protein powders, creatine, stimulants and fat burners.

When we look at these five principles and how they impact your diet, we can easily identify "Caloric Balance" as the most important factor. It should be no surprise that if you want to see any changes – be it gain muscle or lose fat – caloric balance should always be considered first. Fortunately, all you really have to remember is common sense: "Eat less and you will lose weight, eat more and you will gain weight."

A proper calorie consumption accounts for about half of your results and if we also look at macronutrient intake, 80% of a successful diet is already covered. This means that these four factors - calories, protein, carbohydrates, and fats -mostly determine whether you will reach your dietary goals or not. Nutrient timing, food composition and supplements play a minor role in overall results and many of their effects are oftentimes exaggerated by the fitness industry.

Macronutrients Explained

Now that we know how important macronutrients are for your diet, let's look at some ways we can best integrate them into our diet. The most important macronutrients are carbohydrates, protein, fats and water. Carbs, fats and protein are interchangeable as sources of energy, with fats yielding nine calories per gram, and protein and carbohydrates both yielding four calories per gram.

Unlike macronutrients, our bodies need the so-called micronutrients (vitamins and trace minerals) only in very small amounts. Vitamins are organic substances that we ingest with our foods, which act like catalysts, substances that help to trigger other reactions in the body. Trace minerals are inorganic substances, which play a role in several metabolic processes, and contribute to the synthesis of such elements as protein, glycogen and fats.

Carbohydrates ("carbs"):

Despite what many people want you to believe, carbs are not evil. They are an important source of energy for your body. The problem is that the average person over-consumes certain sources of carbohydrates, usually simple sugars from candy and soda, while forgetting about the complex carbs found in brown rice, sweet potatoes and oats. These are especially important for hardgainers, since you need to make sure to cover your daily calorie requirements through healthy foods, which your body can actually process.

<u>Good Sources of Carbohydrate:</u>

- Vegetables (all kinds)
- Fruit
- Oats and oatmeal
- Brown Rice
- Seeds
- Nuts
- Quinoa
- Chia
- Yams
- Lentils

- Whole Grain Breads
- Whole Grain Pitas
- Whole Grain Cereals
- (Sweet) Potatoes
- Whole grain pastas
- Beans

<u>Carbohydrates to limit or avoid:</u>

- White Pasta
- White Rice
- White Bread
- Instant Oatmeal
- Fruit Juices
- Bagels
- Donuts
- Muffins
- Sweets and Candies
- Processed Breakfast Cereals
- Processed corn products
- Processed potato products
- Processed rice products

Proteins:

Protein is a linked chain of amino acids, necessary for your body to maintain, grow and repair damage to its muscles. The normal adult gets enough protein through a healthy diet of natural foods, though an intense exercise program like the one in this book will call for a higher protein intake and the use of protein shakes for optimal results. Even though we already learned that supplements have a relatively small impact on your diet results, I do believe a good protein powder should be part of an athlete's diet.

There are various myths about protein shakes, such as they are bad for your kidneys. While there might have been a few cases of kidney problems due to the excessive use of protein supplements, all you need to do to avoid this problem is drink more water. Excess protein will be flushed out of your kidneys and you will simply pee it out. Another popular discussion in the bodybuilding scene regards the amount of protein you need to consume in order to build muscle. Research has shown that the average trainee looking to build muscle should consume between 0.6g and 1.1g of protein per pound of bodyweight. The exact amount depends on your genetics, goals and the rest of your diet, but you should aim to hit somewhere in that range.

Good Sources of Protein:

- Fish (Tuna, Salmon, Halibut)
- Lean Chicken (Chicken Breast)
- Cheese (Non-fat Mozzarella)
- Lean Beef and Veal (Low Fat)
- Pork Loin (Chops)
- Yogurt, Milk, and Soymilk
- Beans (Mature Soy Beans)
- Eggs (Especially Egg Whites)
- Nuts and Seeds (Pumpkin, Squash, and Watermelon Seeds)

Disclaimer: Animal products such as meat, eggs and dairy are good sources of protein; however, they can also be high in saturated fat and cholesterol. That is why more and more bodybuilders switch to a vegetarian or even vegan diet. Here are a few good vegetarian and vegan sources of protein:

- Green peas
- Quinoa
- Nuts and nut butter
- Beans
- Chickpeas
- Tempeh and tofu

- Edamame
- Leafy greens
- Hemp

Fats:

Just like calories, fats are not evil, per se. Instead, they perform a variety of necessary functions in your body. The problem is that most people eat too many saturated fats and trans fats, which increase LDL ("bad") cholesterol and decrease HDL ("good") cholesterol, while eating too few healthy fats like monounsaturated fats (found in canola oil and olive oil) and Omega-3 fatty acids (found in flax seed oil, fish and other sources). The fact that fats have more calories ounce-for-ounce than proteins and carbohydrates is important for hardgainers. A diet which includes healthy fats will help you pack on size much quicker than any low fat diet.

Good Sources of Healthy Fats:

- Avocados
- Eggs
- Olive Oil
- Nuts
- Nut Butter
- Fatty Fish
- Dark Chocolate (in moderate amounts)
- Coconuts and Coconut Oil

Fatty Foods to limit or avoid:

- Pizza
- Burgers
- Microwaved Popcorn
- French Fries
- Frozen Foods
- Cookies
- Potato Chips

Other Supplements

Besides the already mentioned protein powder, there are two major kinds of supplements that can help you get more out of your workouts. Most others fall in the "marketing department", meaning their small benefitsdon't justify their price.

<u>Creatine</u>

Creatine monohydrate is an organic acid found naturally in food. It exists in substantial quantities in meats like beef and fish. As a supplement, creatine is widely accepted as offering relatively direct benefits to both general athletes and bodybuilders alike, which is why it is one of the most widely used supplements on the market. It will help you reduce muscle soreness after a workout, build muscle and improve strength. Some people believe that creatine causes kidney problems, but these claims have been disproven by countless studies. For healthy athletes, creatine has been shown to have no harmful side effects and only subjects that already suffered from kidney diseases before the trials reported problems from the creatine.

Pre-Workout Booster

A good pre-workout drink can take your training to a new level. A bad one can be dangerous and will waste your money. The problem is that most pre-workout supplements rely on stimulants and fail to supply real nutrients to muscle fibers. When buying a booster, you should always check the ingredients! Here is a list of the most common ingredients and how they affect your body. If you see something in you pre-workout that is not on the list, be sure to check for possible side effects:

Amino acids: Provide fuel for your muscles during workout; essential for muscle recovery and synthesis.

Beta-alanine: Increases power in muscle contraction by forming the double amino acid protein carnosine; enhances muscle strength during workout.

Betaine: A modified amino acid and beet derivative; possible strength boost of up to 25%.

B Vitamins: Helps in the pre-workout energy production.

Caffeine: Improves muscle endurance and lessens soreness; allows for harder training.

Creatine: See above.

DMAE: Improve mood, mental function, and muscular strength by increasing choline in the brain.

Glutamine: Increase growth hormone levels; reduces fatigue and stabilizes endurance.

Green Tea Extract: Improves fat burning and works as a natural stimulant.

Taurine: Similar to caffeine; improves muscular endurance by up to 50%.

Note: All pre-workout drinks should be cycled! A booster should be used for 6 - 8 weeks, followed by a break of 2 - 3 weeks.

Applying The 80/20 Rule To Recovery

Besides your diet and training, recovery is the most important factor to building muscle and a stronger physique in general. Whether or not you will achieve your fitness goals depends on these three factors.

Muscle growth is a very logical process. The training itself is only the trigger (stimulus) for muscle growth. During a workout you overload your muscles and break down muscle fibers. Under the right conditions, they will grow back larger in order to withstand higher workloads in your next training. It is important to note that your muscles do not grow during the workout, but afterwards! The body builds stronger muscle fibers only when it has time to recover and this is done for the most part while you sleep.

Applying the 80/20 Rule to recovery means that you should achieve at least 80% of your necessary recovery during sleep hours. How? By getting at least seven to nine hours of uninterrupted sleep per night. Anything below seven hours and you will sacrifice possible muscle gains. If you are under a lot of stress or find it hard to sleep that long, try to take regular naps throughout the day.

There are other ways to maximize your recovery ability like massages, meditating and even prescription drugs. However, they usually fall into the category of things that yield only 20% results with 80% of the effort.

The 80/20 Rule In Bodybuilding - Summary

The 80/20 Rule states that you can achieve 80% of the results with only 20% of the input. By implementing the principlesin this book regardingexercise, nutrition and recovery, you can build muscle and lose fat more efficiently and with less effort.

When exercising, try to concentrate onheavy compound lifts that involve several muscle groups at once. They will build the majority of your muscle mass and work capacity. My list of the best compound exercises will help you put together the perfect workout.

Your diet plans should focus on the proper caloric and macronutrient intake, as these two factors will primarily drive physique changes. Supplements and meal timing complement your diet but should never be its center.

For optimal recovery, sleep at least seven to nine hours per night and/or take regular naps. Uninterrupted sleep is by far the most effectiveway of ensuringproper recovery.

All Exercises Explained:

This chapter explains every exercise mentioned above in detail with safety tips and possible variations. If you want to learn about the best exercises for all your muscle groups, check out my other book *"The Gym Bible"*

Chest

Bench Press

Main Muscle: Chest (Upper and lower pectorals)
Secondary Muscles: Shoulders, Triceps
Equipment: Barbell, Dumbbells (see variations)
Exercise Type: Compound
Force: Push

1. Setup
With your eyes under the bar, lie supine on the bench. Lift your chest and squeeze your shoulder blades. Your feet should be flat on the floor.

2. Grip
Place each pinky on the ring marks of your bar. Your grip should be medium-width grip (creating a 90-degree angle in the middle of the movement between your forearms and upper arms). Hold the bar in the base of your palm with straight wrists and a full grip.

3. Unrack
Take a big breath and dismount the barbell by straightening your arms. Move it over your shoulders, keeping your elbows locked.

4. Lower the bar
Lower the barbell to your chest. Your elbows should be at a 75° angle, while keeping your forearms vertical. Hold your breath at the bottom.

5. Press
Press the barbell upward until your arms are extended. The proper form is pressing the bar in a diagonal line from shoulders to chest and back up. This increases the distance, but prevents shoulder impingement. Your butt must also stay on the bench. Lock your elbows at the top and breathe.

Tips & Safety

- Don't let the bar drift too far forward. It should touch your middle chest and nowhere else.

- Never bounce the bar off your chest. You should always be in control of the weight.

- If you find yourself without a spotter, use a power rack. They have horizontal safety pins to catch the bar if you fail.

- Don't Bench Press using the "suicide grip" (thumbless grip). The barbell can slip out of your hands and drop on your chest.

Variations

Close Grip Bench Press:
This variation uses a narrow grip. You set up your flat bench like you do for the regular Bench Press, but this time, your grip is only about shoulder-width apart. Then lower the barbell to your chest. Close Grip Bench Press is harder than medium grip, because your (usually weaker) triceps work harder while your chest works less.

Wide Grip Bench Press:
This variation uses a wider than normal grip. You set up your flat bench like you do for the regular Bench Press. Your grip should be around three inches away from shoulder width for each hand. Then lower the barbell to your chest. Compared to a narrower grip, the wide grip works the pectoralis major more intensely and causes greater activity in the anterior deltoid.

Incline Bench Press

Main Muscle: Upper Chest (Pectoralis Major, Clavicular)
Secondary Muscles: Shoulders, Triceps
Equipment: Barbell, Dumbbells (see variations)
Exercise Type: Compound
Force: Push

1. Setup
With your eyes under the bar, lie on an incline bench. Lift your chest and squeeze your shoulder blades. Your feet should be flat on the floor.

2. Grip
Place each pinky on the ring marks of your bar. Your grip should be medium-width grip (creating a 90-degree angle in the middle of the movement between your forearms and upper arms). Hold the bar in the base of your palm with straight wrists and a full grip.

3. Unrack
Take a big breath and dismount the barbell by straightening your arms. Move it over your shoulders, keeping your elbows locked.

4. Lower the bar
Lower the barbell to your upper chest. Hold your breath at the bottom.

5. Press
Press the barbell upward until your arms are extended. Squeeze your chest in the contracted position. Your butt must also stay on the bench. Lock your elbows at the top and breathe.

Tips & Safety

- Don't let the bar drift too far forward. It should touch your upper chest and nowhere else.

- Never bounce the bar off your chest. You should always be in control of the weight.

- If you find yourself without a spotter, use the smith machine. You will be able to lock in the bar at any height if you fail.

- Keep your shoulders and back flat on the bench and your abs drawn in throughout the exercise.

Variations

Wide & Close Grip: See normal Bench Press

Decline Bench Press

Main Muscle: Lower Chest (Pectoralis Major, Sternal)
Secondary Muscles: Shoulders, Triceps
Equipment: Barbell, Dumbbells (see variations)
Exercise Type: Compound
Force: Push

1. Setup
Lie on a decline bench. Your head should be lower than your feet (lock your feet under the pads at the front of the bench). Lift your chest and squeeze your shoulder blades.

2. Grip
Place each pinky on the ring marks of your bar. Your grip should be medium-width grip (creating a 90-degree angle in the middle of the movement between your forearms and upper arms). Hold the bar in the base of your palm with straight wrists and a full grip.

3. Unrack
Take a big breath and dismount the barbell by straightening your arms. Move it over your shoulders, keeping your elbows locked.

4. Lower the bar
Lower the barbell to the lower chest. Hold your breath at the bottom.

5. Press
Exhale and press the barbell upward until your arms are extended. Squeeze your chest in the contracted position. Lock your elbows at the top and breathe.

Tips & Safety

- Unlike the traditional Bench Press, the Decline Bench Press involves less rotation at the shoulders, thus preventing impingement.

- Due to the angle of the decline Bench Press, you will be able to lift more weight. This will stimulate the larger fibers of your muscles, which may have a small positive effect on your ability to build strength and size.

- Don't let the bar drift too far forward. It should touch your upper chest and nowhere else.

- Never bounce the bar off your chest. You should always be in control of the weight.

- Keep your shoulders and back flat on the bench and your abs drawn in throughout the exercise.

Variations

Wide & Close Grip: See normal Bench Press

Back

Deadlift

Main Muscle: Lower Back (Erector Spinae)
Secondary Muscles: Calves, Glutes, Hamstrings, Forearms, Lats, Quadriceps, Traps
Equipment: Barbell
Exercise Type: Compound
Force: Pull

1. Setup

Set upthe barbell with appropriate weight. Don't lift too heavy if you have no experience with this exercise. It can be dangerous.

2. Position

Bend your knees while keeping your back as straight as possible. Bend forward and grasp the bar with an overhand grip. Your hands should be shoulder width apart. Some people have trouble holding on to the bar with this grip. You can also use the mixed grip (one palm facing up, one palm facing down).

3. Execution

While breathing out, push with your legs and get your torso to the upright position. At the top, stick your chest out and pull your shoulders back. Return to the initial position by bending at the knees and leaning the torso forward at the waist. Your back should be kept straight until the weights on the bar touch the floor.

Tips & Safety

- Focus more on your form and less on the weight. During your first workouts, practice the exercise with proper form and light weights. As your confidence grows, you can increase the weight.

- Don't look up while deadlifting. Your body should form a straight line from the top of your head to your lower back.

- Don't do this exercise if you have back issues, it will make them worse.

- Keep your back straight at all times. Lower back rounding or excess arching puts your spine at risk of serious injury.

Lat Pulldown

Main Muscle: Back (latissimusdorsi)
Secondary Muscles: Biceps, Middle Back, Shoulders
Equipment: Cable
Exercise Type: Compound
Force: Pull

1. Setup

Set up the pull-down machine with awide bar attached to the cable. When sitting down, make sure to adjust the knee-padaccording to your height.

2. Position

Using a wide grip, grab the bar with your palms facing forward. With your arms extended and holding the bar, lean back around 30 degrees and stick your chest out.

3. Execution

While breathing out, pull down the bar until it touches your upper chest. The pulling is done primarily with your back muscles rather than your biceps. Draw your shoulders and upper arms down and back while bringing down the weight. Keep your upper body stable during the exercise. Pause for a moment and then return the bar to the original position. Repeat

Tips & Safety

- Use slow and controlled movements and make sure you do not cheat by swinging your back.

- Many bodybuilders avoid pulling down the weight behind the neck, as it can be hard on the rotator cuff due to the hyperextension created.

- Do not hunch over or drop your shoulders.

Bent Over Barbell Row

Main Muscle: Middle Back
Secondary Muscles: Biceps, Lats, Shoulders
Equipment: Barbell
Exercise Type: Compound
Force: Pull

1. Setup
Set upthe barbell with appropriate weight.

2. Position
Hold the barbell with your palms facing down and bend your knees slightly. While keeping the back straight, bring your torso forward. Legs and upper body should create a 100 – 120 degree angle (back almost parallel to the floor). The barbell should now hang directly in front of you.

3. Execution
While breathing out, pull up the barbell. Your elbows should be kept close to your body. Make sure to keep the torso stationary and squeeze your back muscles at the top. Inhale and then lower the barbell back to the starting position. Repeat.

Tips & Safety

- Make sure that you keep the head up during the entire exercise.

- Don't do this exercise if you have back issues, it will make them worse.

- If your lower back gets rounded due to tight hamstrings, either try bending your knees more or don't position the torso as low.

Pull-up

Muscle: Back (latissimusdorsi)
Secondary Muscle: Biceps
Equipment: Body
Exercise Type: Compound
Force: Pull

1. Position

Using a wider than shoulder-width grip, grab the pull-up bar with the palms facing forward.
With your arms extended and holding the bar, bring back your torso around 30 degrees and stick your chest out.

2. Execution

While breathing out, pull your upper body up until it touches your chest by drawing the upper arms and the shoulders down and back. The pulling is done primarily with your back muscles rather than your biceps. Draw your shoulders and upper arms down and back while raising your torso. Pause for a moment and then return to the original position. Repeat.

Tips & Safety

- Your forearms should not move and only hold the bar.

- If you don't have enough strength to perform this exercise, ask a spotter to hold your legs or use a chin-assist machine

- By using a weight belt, you can increase the difficulty

Variations

Hand placement:
-Pronated grip (palms face away from you)
-Supinated grip (palms facing you)
- Mixed grip (one palm facing away, 1 palm facing you)

Other:

- Climber pull-up: Pull yourself up towards one hand.

- Alternating Climber pull-up: Pull yourself up towards onehand. Stay at the position, and move your body towards the other hand and lower yourself.

- Uneven pull-up: Hang a towel over the bar and grab it with one hand. Grab the bar with the other hand. Pull yourself up until your chin is just over the bar.

Legs

Barbell Squat

Main Muscle: Quadriceps
Secondary Muscles: Calves, Glutes, Hamstrings, Lower Back
Equipment: Barbell
Exercise Type: Compound
Force: Push

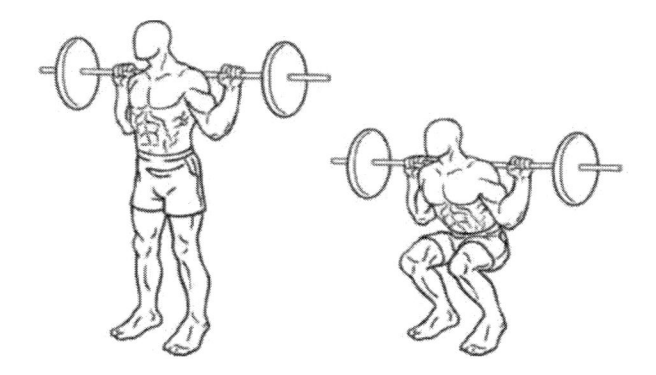

1. Setup

Load the bar with the desiredweight and set it on a rack to just below shoulder level.

2. Position

Step under the bar and place it slightly below the neck, across the back of your shoulders. Grab the bar using aslightly wider than shoulder-width grip. Lift the bar off the rack by pushing with your legs and then straightening your torso. Place your legs in a medium stance (feet shoulder width apart); your toes should be slightly pointed out.

3. Execution

Bend your knees and slowly lower the bar. While inhaling, descend until your thighs are just past parallel to the floor. Then raise the bar as you exhale. Imagine pushing the floor with the heel of your foot as you straighten your legs. Repeat.

Tips & Safety

- Keep your head facing forward and your back straight at all times.

- Watch out for equal distribution of weight throughout your forefoot and heel.

- If you have back issues, substitute the exercise with the dumbbell squat variation.

Leg Press

Main Muscle: Quadriceps
Secondary Muscles: Calves, Glutes, Hamstrings
Equipment: Machine
Exercise Type: Compound
Force: Push

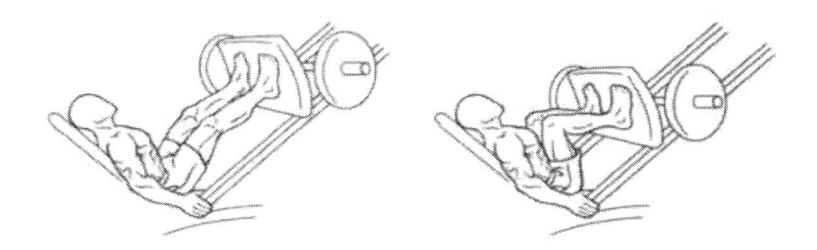

1. Setup

Load the machine with the desired weight.

2. Position

Sit down on the machine and place your legs on the platform in front of you. Your feet should be about shoulder width apart. Release the dock lever, grasp the handles to your sides and press the platform all the way up until your legs are fully extended.

3. Execution

While inhaling, lower the platform until your upper and lower legs create a 90-degree angle. Then, push back the platform to the original position, using the heels of your feet and your quadriceps. Exhale during this movement. Repeat.

Tips & Safety

- Don't lock your knees at the top.

- You should keep your knees pointed in the same direction as your feet.

- Placing your feet slightly higher on the platform will emphasize the Gluteus Maximus. Placing them lower emphasizes Quadriceps.

Dumbbell Lunges

Main Muscle: Quadriceps
Secondary Muscles: Calves, Glutes, Hamstrings
Equipment: Dumbbell
Exercise Type: Compound
Force: Push

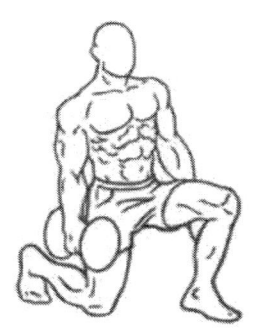

1. Position

Stand with two dumbbells in your hands as seen in the picture.

2. Execution

Step forward with one leg. Land first on your heel, then forefoot. Lower your body by flexing the hip and knee of the front leg until the knee of the rear leg almost touches the floor. While exhaling, push up and go back to the original position. Use mainly the heel for this movement. Repeat by alternating lunge with opposite legs.

Tips & Safety

- Don't allow the knee of your front leg to go beyond your toes as you lower your body. This will stress your knee joint.

- Remember to keep your front shin perpendicular to the ground.

- Avoid this exercise if you have balance problems.

Variations

Static Lunges: Using only one leg, go up and down from the starting position. Later switch the leg and do the same.

Walking Lunges: Instead of returning to the starting position, walk across the room in a lunging fashion.

Using a Barbell: This variation should be used by experienced athletes with no balance issues.

Shoulders

Seated Barbell Military Press / Shoulder Press

Main Muscle: Shoulders
Secondary Muscles: Triceps
Equipment: Barbell
Exercise Type: Compound
Force: Push

1. Setup
Sit on a Military Press Bench with the bar in front of you on the rack.

2. Position
Carefully pick up the bar with a slightly wider than shoulder width grip (palms facing forward). Lift it over your head by extending your arms. Stop at about shoulder level (the bar should be slightly in front of your head).

3. Execution
While inhaling, lower the bar down to your upper chest. Then lift it back up to the original position. Exhale while doing this movement.

Tips & Safety

- Make sure to set the barbell slightly below shoulder height so itcan be more easily unracked.

- Your range of motion will be compromised if your grip is too wide.

- Always keep your back straight to not lose control of the weight.

Variation

- Military Press can also be performed standing up, however. If you have lower back problems,you should usethe seated variety.

- You can lower the bar behind the neck, but this may cause shoulder problems, as it can be hard on the rotator cuff due to the hyperextension created.

Arms

Chin Up

Main Muscle: Biceps
Secondary Muscles: Forearms, Lats, Middle Back
Equipment: Body
Exercise Type: Compound
Force: Pull

1. Position

Using a closer than shoulder-width grip, grab the pull-up bar with the palms facing inward.

With your arms extended and holding the bar, bring back your torso around 30 degrees and stick your chest out.

2. Execution

While breathing out, pull your upper body up until your head is around the level of the pull-up bar. The pulling is done primarily with your biceps. Keep your elbows close to your body. Pause for a moment and then return to the original position. Repeat.

Tips & Safety

- Your forearms should do no other work other than hold the bar.

- If you don't have enough strength to perform this exercise, ask a spotter to hold your legs or use a chin assist machine.

- By using a weight belt, you can increase the difficulty.

Variations

Hand placement:
-Pronated grip(palms face away from you).
-Supinated grip(palms facing you).
- Mixed grip (one palm facing away, 1 palm facing you).

Triceps Dip

Main Muscle: Triceps
Secondary Muscles: Chest, Shoulders
Equipment: Body
Exercise Type: Compound
Force: Push

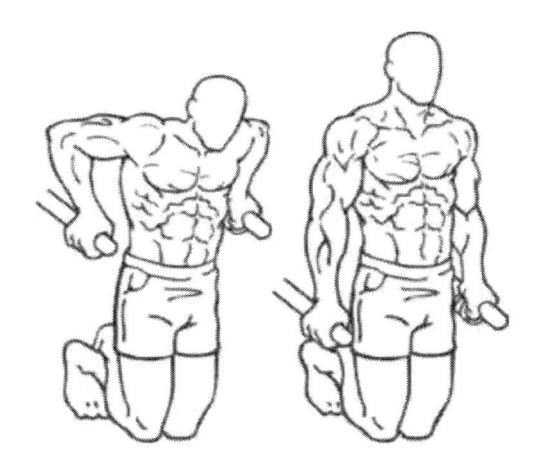

1. Position

With your arms almost locked, hold your body above the bars.

2. Execution

While inhaling, slowly lower yourself downwarduntil there is a 90-degree angle formed between the upper arm and forearm. Your upper body should remain upright while keeping your elbows close to your body. While exhaling, push your body back to the original position using your triceps. Repeat.

Tips & Safety

- If you don't have enough strength to perform this exercise, ask a spotter to hold your legs or use a dip assist machine.

- By using a weight belt, you can increase the difficulty.

Variations

- Dips can be done as either a triceps or a chest exercise. The more you lean forward while performing the exercise, the more your chest will be involved.

Other Books By Felix Harder

Click On The Cover To Go To The Book

If you enjoyed this book, please consider leaving a review on Amazon. Reviews help us authors out a lot and I would love to know what you thought about my work.

Sincerely

Felix Harder

Made in the USA
Lexington, KY
06 November 2016